**REDCAR &
CLEVELAND
COLLEGE**

Sir William Turner
Learning Resource Centre
Redcar & Cleveland College

This item is due for return on or before the last date shown below
If for any reason you are unable to return by this date it may be
possible to renew your loan by email: lrc@cleveland.ac.uk
or phone 01642 473132 ext

History Makers

Winston Churchill

and the Second World War.

Sarah Ridley

W
FRANKLIN WATTS
LONDON•SYDNEY

First published in 2009 by
Franklin Watts
338 Euston Road
London NW1 3BH

Franklin Watts Australia
Hachette Children's Books
Level 17/207 Kent Street
Sydney

ISBN 978 0 7496 8708 3
Dewey classification: 941.082'092

Series Editor: Jeremy Smith
Art director: Jonathan Hair
Design: Simon Morse
Cover Design: Jonathan Hair
Picture research: Sarah Ridley

Picture credits: AKG Images: 13.
Bettmann/Corbis: 19. Mary Evans PL: 15.
Fotomas/Topfoto: 9. Fox/Hulton
Archive/Getty Images: 23. Hulton
Archive/Getty Images: front cover 1, 5, 7,
8, 11, 12, 14. Hulton Deutsch/Corbis: 16.
Keystone/Topfoto: front cover r, 1.
Picturepoint/Topham: 18, 21.
Popperfoto/Getty Images: 10, 20.
Sambraus/AKG Images: 4.
Frank Scherschel/Time Life/Getty Images:
22. Topfoto: 6. World History
Archive/Topfoto: 17.

A CIP catalogue record for this book is
available from the British Library

Franklin Watts is a division of Hachette
Children's Books, an Hachette UK
company.
www.hachette.co.uk

Printed in China

Contents

The Churchill family

Winston Churchill was born on 30th November, 1874. His father was an English lord and his mother was a rich American.

Winston was born at his grandparent's home, Blenheim Palace, near Oxford.

1837 ▶

Queen Victoria comes to the throne.

Winston's family home was in London. His father was a Member of Parliament, and both his parents lived very busy lives. Winston did not see much of his parents but he did grow very fond of his nanny.

A photo of Winston's father, Lord Randolph Churchill.

1874 ▶

Lord Randolph Churchill becomes a Member of Parliament (MP).

30 November
1874 ▶

Winston is born.

Childhood

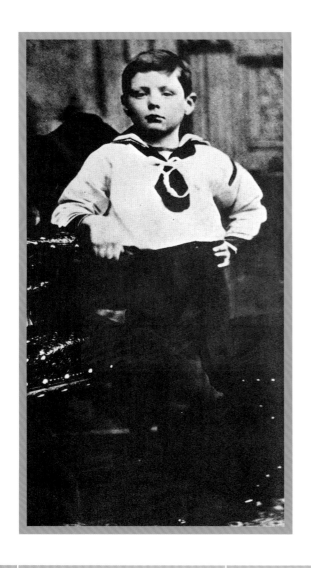

When Winston was four, the family moved to Ireland. A few years later there was a new baby brother for Winston, called Jack.

◀ Winston as a young boy.

1877	February 1880	June 1880
The Churchill family moves to Ireland.	Jack Churchill is born.	The Churchill family returns to London.

Jack and Winston, on each side of their mother in 1889.

At the age of eight, Winston's parents sent him to boarding school. He hated it and, after two years, he moved to a different school. There he took and passed an exam for a famous school called Harrow.

1882 ▶
Winston goes to boarding school.

1887 ▶
Queen Victoria's Golden Jubilee.

From school to college

The teachers at Harrow School praised Winston's work in English and history. They were not as pleased with his maths, or his timekeeping.

▲ Winston in school uniform. He missed his parents when he was away at school.

1888 ▶

Winston starts at Harrow School.

Winston in his army uniform.

Winston decided he wanted to be a soldier. After leaving school, he went to army college and he did well. Now he took his first army job in India.

1893 ▶

Winston starts at army college (called Sandhurst).

1895 ▶

Winston leaves army college. His father and his nanny die.

9

Adventures abroad

Britain ruled over a huge empire which stretched across the world. The British army helped to protect the Empire. As a soldier in India, Winston was part of this.

Winston was a cavalry officer, a soldier on horseback.

1896 ▶

Winston goes to India.

After India he went to fight in Sudan. Alongside his army life, Winston earned money by writing newspaper reports and history books.

 Winston took part in the Battle of Omdurman in Sudan.

1898 ▶
Winston goes to Sudan. The British army win the war there.

1899 ▶
The Boer War begins in South Africa.

Into politics

After a few more adventures abroad, Winston decided that he wanted to be a politician. In 1900 he became a Member of Parliament (MP).

▶ In 1908 Winston married Clementine. They had five children.

1900 ▶
Winston becomes a Conservative Member of Parliament (MP).

1901 ▶
Queen Victoria dies. Edward VII is crowned.

1905 ▶
Winston becomes a Liberal MP.

Winston made one big mistake during the war, which resulted in thousands of soldiers dying at Gallipoli in Turkey.

In 1914, the First World War started. During the war, Winston held some important jobs in the government and fought as a soldier for a short time.

1908 ▶

Winston and Clementine marry.

1910 ▶

Edward VII dies. George V is now king.

1914 ▶

First World War breaks out.

The family home

When the First World War ended in 1918, Winston continued as an MP. He shared his time between London and his country home.

Winston enjoyed building walls. Two of his children, Sarah and Mary, are helping here at their home, Chartwell, in Kent.

1918

The First World War ends.

1922

Winston and Clementine buy Chartwell, a house in Kent.

During the 1930s Winston began to worry about a man called Adolf Hitler who was gaining power in Germany. Winston feared he would start another world war.

Adolf Hitler became the leader of Germany in 1933.

1924 ▶

Winston changes back to the Conservative Party.

1933 ▶

Adolf Hitler becomes the German Chancellor.

15

The Second World War

In 1939, the German army invaded Poland. This led to Britain and France declaring war on Germany. The next year, Winston became the British Prime Minister.

Winston gave many speeches on the radio and thousands listened.

1936 ▶

George V dies. Edward VIII is followed by George VI.

1939 ▶

The Second World War begins.

British soldiers wade into the sea from French beaches after the German invasion.

The war was not going well for Britain. Germany had invaded several countries, including France. Winston gave speeches and worked long hours to inspire the British people to keep fighting the Germans.

10 May

1940 ▶

Winston becomes Prime Minister at the age of 65.

1940 ▶

Germany invades many countries.

May 26 - June 4

1940 ▶

British troops are rescued from Dunkirk in France.

Battle of Britain

Some German aeroplanes during the Battle of Britain.

In the summer of 1940, Hitler ordered the German air force to bomb British ports and airfields. For three months the Royal Air Force fought the Germans and beat them.

June
1940 ▶

Italy joins the war on the German side.

Winston visited bombed cities, including Coventry.

However, Hitler could not be stopped that easily. He gave the order to bomb British cities instead. He wanted to make Britain surrender.

1940 ▶

The Battle of Britain. The British and German airforces battle in the air.

1940-1941 ▶

Air-raids on British cities.

War around the world

In 1941, Russia and the United States joined the war and battles raged around the world. Winston kept the British people strong, even when the news was bad.

▶ Winston flew around the world to encourage British soldiers and sailors.

1941 ▶
Russia and the USA enter the war.

1942 ▶
Japan wins many battles.

1944 ▶
D-Day Landings. A million US and British troops invade France.

After five long years, the war ended in 1945. Germany had lost. Now the British people wanted a change and Winston lost his position as Prime Minister.

Winston waves to the crowds on VE Day, the day the war ended in Europe.

June
1945 ▶
The Second World War ends.

July
1945 ▶
Winston replaced by Clement Attlee as Prime Minister.

June
1947 ▶
India gains independence from Britain.

21

Last years

Winston became Prime Minister once more in 1951. After four years he left this job but he remained a Member of Parliament almost until his death.

▲ Winston enjoyed painting on holiday, and at home.

1951	**1952**	June **1953**
Winston becomes Prime Minister, aged 76.	George VI dies. Elizabeth II becomes queen.	Coronation of Elizabeth II.

London came to a halt as Winston's coffin was pulled through the streets.

In old age Winston travelled, wrote books, painted and spent time with his large family. He died in 1965 at the age of 90. Remembered as one of the greatest British leaders, his funeral was watched by millions.

December
1953 ▶
Winston wins the Nobel Prize for Literature.

1955 ▶
Winston resigns as Prime Minister.

24 January
1965
Winston dies, aged 90.

Glossary

Air-raid A bomb attack from aeroplanes.

Boarding school A school where children stay during term time.

Cavalry Soldiers who fight on horseback.

Conservative Party One of the main political parties.

Coronation When a king or queen is crowned.

First World War The world war between 1914 and 1918.

Golden Jubilee The celebration held to mark 50 years of a king or queen's reign.

Hitler Adolf Hitler was the leader of the German National Socialist (Nazi) Party.

Liberal Party One of the main political parties.

Member of Parliament A person elected by voters to represent them in the House of Commons.

Nanny Someone paid to look after the children in a wealthy family.

Prime Minister The leader of the government.

RAF The name given to Britain's Royal Air Force.

Second World War The world war between 1939 and 1945.

Index